卞尺丹几乙し丹卞と
Translated Language Learning

The Country of the Blind
盲人之国
H.G. Wells

English / 普通话

Copyright © 2024 Tranzlaty
All rights reserved.
Published by Tranzlaty
ISBN: 978-1-83566-237-3
Original text by H.G. Wells
The Country of the Blind
First published in English in 1904
www.tranzlaty.com

Three hundred miles and more from Chimborazo
距钦博拉索三百英里以上
one hundred miles from the snows of Cotopaxi
距科托帕希的雪地一百英里
in the wildest wastes of Ecuador's Andes
在厄瓜多尔安第斯山脉最荒凉的荒原上
cut off from all the world of men
与所有男人的世界隔绝
there lies the mysterious mountain valley
那里是神秘的山谷
the Country of the Blind
盲人之国
Long years ago, that valley was open to the world
很久以前,那个山谷向世界开放
men came through frightful gorges and over an icy pass
人们穿过可怕的峡谷,越过冰冷的山口
from there they could get into the valley's equable meadows
从那里,他们可以进入山谷中平等的草地
and men did indeed come to the valley this way
人们确实以这种方式来到山谷
some families of Peruvian half-breeds came
一些秘鲁混血儿的家庭来了
they were fleeing from the tyranny of an evil Spanish ruler
他们正在逃离邪恶的西班牙统治者的暴政
Then came the stupendous outbreak of Mindobamba
然后是明多班巴的惊人爆发
it was night in Quito for seventeen days
在基多度过了十七天的夜晚
and the water was boiling at Yaguachi
Yaguachi的水沸腾了
the fish were dying as far as Guayaquil

鱼一直死到瓜亚基尔
everywhere along the Pacific slopes there were land-slips
太平洋斜坡上到处都是山体滑坡
and there was swift thawings and sudden floods
还有迅速的解冻和突如其来的洪水
one whole side of the old Arauca crest slipped
旧阿劳卡峰的整侧滑落
it all came down in a thunderous moment
这一切都在雷鸣般的时刻降临
this cut off access to the Country of the Blind for ever
这永远切断了进入盲人之国的通道
the exploring feet of men wondered that way no more
探索的人们的脚不再这样想了
But one of these early settlers happened to be close by
但这些早期定居者中的一位恰好就在附近
he was on the other side of the gorges that day
那天他在峡谷的另一边
the day that the world had so terribly shaken itself
世界如此可怕地动摇自己的一天
he had to forget his wife and his children
他不得不忘记他的妻子和孩子
and he had to forget all his friends and possessions
他不得不忘记他所有的朋友和财产
and he had to start life over again
他不得不重新开始生活
a new life in the lower world
下层世界的新生活
but illness and blindness took hold of him
但疾病和失明抓住了他
and he died of punishment in the mines
他在矿井中死于惩罚
but the story he told begot a legend
但他讲述的故事催生了一个传奇

a legend that lingers to this day
一个流传至今的传奇
and it travels the length of Andes
它穿越了安第斯山脉的长度
He told of his reason for venturing back from that fastness
他讲述了他从这种快感中冒险回来的原因
the place into which he had been carried
他被抬进去的地方
he had been taken to that place as a child
他小时候被带到那个地方
lashed to a llama, beside a vast bale of gear
鞭打在骆驼身上，旁边是一大捆装备
He said the valley had all that the heart of man could desire
他说，山谷里有人类内心所渴望的一切
sweet water, pasture, an even climate
甘甜的水，牧场，均匀的气候
slopes of rich brown soil and tangles of a shrub
肥沃的棕色土壤和灌木的缠结的斜坡
he spoke of bushes that bore an excellent fruit
他谈到了结出极好果实的灌木丛
on one side there were great hanging forests of pine
一边是巨大的松树林
the pine had held the avalanches high
这棵松树高高举起了雪崩
Far overhead, on three sides, there were vast cliffs
在远处的头顶上，三面都是巨大的悬崖
they were of a grey-green rock
它们是一块灰绿色的岩石
and at the top there were caps of ice
在顶部有冰帽
but the glacier stream came not to them
但冰川溪流并没有来到他们身边

it flowed away by the farther slopes
它从更远的山坡上流走了
and only now and then huge ice masses fell
只是时不时地巨大的冰块掉下来
In this valley it neither rained nor snowed
在这个山谷里，既不下雨也不下雪
but the abundant springs gave a rich green pasture
但丰富的泉水给了一个丰富的绿色牧场
their irrigation spread over all the valley space
他们的灌溉遍布整个山谷空间
The settlers there did well indeed
那里的定居者确实做得很好
Their beasts did well and multiplied
他们的野兽做得很好，成倍增加
only one thing marred their happiness
只有一件事破坏了他们的幸福
And it was enough to mar their happiness greatly
这足以大大损害他们的幸福
A strange disease had come upon them
一种奇怪的疾病降临在他们身上
it made all their children blind
这使他们所有的孩子都失明了
He was sent to find some charm or antidote
他被派去寻找一些魅力或解毒剂
a cure against this plague of blindness
治愈这种失明的瘟疫
so he returned down the gorge
于是他回到了峡谷
but not without fatigue, danger, and difficulty
但并非没有疲劳、危险和困难
In those days men did not think of germs
在那些日子里，人们没有想到细菌
sin explained why this had happened
沈解释了为什么会发生这种情况

this is what he thought too
他也是这么想的
there was a cause for this affliction
这种痛苦是有原因的
the immigrants had been without a priest
移民们没有牧师
they had failed to set up a shrine
他们没有建立神社
this should have been the first thing they did
这应该是他们做的第一件事
He wanted to build a shrine
他想建一座神社
a handsome, cheap, effectual shrine
一个英俊、廉价、有效的神社
he wanted it to be erected in the valley
他想把它竖立在山谷里
he wanted relics and such-like
他想要遗物之类的东西
he wanted potent things of faith
他想要信心的有力的东西
he wanted blessed objects and mysterious medals
他想要祝福的物品和神秘的奖章
and he felt they needed prayers
他觉得他们需要祷告
In his wallet he had a bar of silver
他的钱包里有一根银条
but he would not say from where it was
但他不会说它来自哪里
he insisted there was no silver in the valley
他坚称山谷里没有银子
and he had the insistence of an inexpert liar
他有一个不专业的骗子的坚持
They had collected their money and ornaments
他们收集了他们的钱和装饰品

he said they had little need for such treasure
他说他们几乎不需要这样的宝藏
he told them he would buy them holy help
他告诉他们，他会给他们买到神圣的帮助
even though this was against their will
即使这违背了他们的意愿
he was sunburnt, gaunt, and anxious
他被晒伤，憔悴而焦虑
he was unused to the ways of the lower world
他不习惯下层世界的方式
clutching his hat feverishly he told his story
他狂热地抓着帽子，讲述了他的故事
he told his story to some keen-eyed priest
他把自己的故事告诉了一位眼光敏锐的神父
he secured some holy remedies
他得到了一些神圣的补救措施
blessed water, statues, crosses and prayer books
祝福水、雕像、十字架和祈祷书
and he sought to return and save his people
他寻求返回并拯救他的人民
he came to the where the gorge had been
他来到了峡谷所在的地方
but in front of him was a mass of fallen stone
但在他面前是一大堆掉落的石头
imagine his infinite dismay
想象一下他无限的沮丧
he had been expelled by nature from his land
他被大自然驱逐出他的土地
But the rest of his story of mischances is lost
但他关于不幸故事的其余部分已经丢失了
all we know of is his evil death after several years
我们所知道的只是他在几年后邪恶的死亡
a poor stray from that remoteness!
一个可怜的流浪者，远离那个遥远的地方！

The stream that had once made the gorge diverted
曾经使峡谷改道的溪流
now it bursts from the mouth of a rocky cave
现在它从一个岩石洞穴的入口中爆发出来
and the legend of his story took on its own life
他的故事的传说有了自己的生命
it developed into the legend one may still hear today
它发展成为人们今天可能仍然听到的传说
a race of blind men "somewhere over there"
"那边某处"的盲人种族
the little population was now isolated
人口稀少，现在被孤立了
the valley was forgotten by the outside world
山谷被外界遗忘了
and their disease ran its course
他们的疾病就这样过去了
The old had to grope to find their way
老人不得不摸索才能找到自己的路
the young could see a little, but dimly
年轻人能看到一点，但很模糊
and the newborns never saw at all
新生儿根本看不见
But life was very easy in the valley
但是在山谷里生活非常轻松
there were neither thorns nor briars
既没有荆棘，也没有荆棘
there were no evil insects in the land
这片土地上没有邪恶的昆虫
and there were no dangerous beasts
而且没有危险的野兽
a gentle breed of llamas grazed the valley
一群温和的骆驼在山谷中放牧
those that could see had become purblind gradually
那些能看到的人逐渐变成了紫瞎

so their loss was scarcely noticed
因此，他们的损失几乎没有被注意到
The elders guided the sightless youngsters
长者引导失明的年轻人
and the young soon knew the whole valley marvellously
年轻人很快就对整个山谷了如指掌
even when the last sight died out, the race lived on
即使最后一幕消失了，比赛仍在继续
There had been enough time to adapt
有足够的时间来适应
they learned the control of fire
他们学会了对火的控制
they carefully put it in stoves of stone
他们小心翼翼地把它放在石炉里
at first they were a simple strain of people
起初，他们是一群简单的人
they had never had books or writing
他们从未有过书籍或写作
and they were only slightly touched by Spanish civilisation
他们只是被西班牙文明所触动
although they had some of the Peruvian traditions and arts
尽管他们有一些秘鲁的传统和艺术
and they kept some of those philosophies alive
他们保留了其中一些哲学
Generation followed generation
一代接一代
They forgot many things from the world
他们忘记了世界上的许多事情
but they also devised many new things
但他们也设计了许多新事物
the greater world they came from became mythical

他们来自的更广阔的世界变成了神话
colours and details were uncertain
颜色和细节不确定
and reference to sight became a metaphor
对视觉的提及成为一种隐喻
In all things apart from sight they were strong and able
在除了视觉之外的所有事情上,他们都是强壮而能干的
occasionally one with an original mind was born to them
偶尔,他们就生了一个有独创心智的人
someone who could talk and persuade
一个会说话和说服的人
These passed away, leaving their effects
这些都过去了,留下了影响
and the little community grew in numbers
这个小社区的数量也在增长
and their understanding of their world grew
他们对世界的理解也越来越深
and they settled social and economic problems that arose
他们解决了出现的社会和经济问题
Generations followed more generations
几代人接踵而至的几代人
fifteen generations had passed since that ancestor left
自从那位祖先离开以来,已经过去了十五代
the ancestor who took the bar of silver
拿走银条的祖先
the ancestor who went to find God's aid
去寻找上帝帮助的祖先
the ancestor who never returned to the valley
再也没有回到山谷的祖先
but fifteen generations later a new man came
但十五代人之后,一个新人来了
a man from the outside world

一个来自外界的男人

a man who happened to find the valley of the blind
一个碰巧找到盲人谷的人

this is the story of that man
这是那个男人的故事

He was a mountaineer from the country near Quito
他是来自基多附近乡村的登山者

a man who had been down to the sea
一个下到海里的人

a man who had seen the world
一个见过世界的人

a reader of books in an original way
以原创方式阅读书籍

an acute and enterprising man
一个敏锐而有进取心的人

he had been taken on by a party of Englishmen
他被一群英国人带走了

they had come out to Ecuador to climb mountains
他们来到厄瓜多尔爬山

he replaced one of their guides who had fallen ill
他取代了一位生病的向导

He had climbed many mountains of the world
他爬过世界上许多山

and then came the attempt at Mount Parascotopetl
然后是帕拉斯科托佩特尔山的尝试

this was the Matterhorn of the Andes
这是安第斯山脉的马特宏峰

here he was lost to the outer world
在这里,他迷失在外面的世界

The story of that accident has been written a dozen times
那次事故的故事已经写了十几遍了

Pointer's narrative is the best account of events
Pointer 的叙述是对事件的最佳描述

He tells about the small group of mountaineers
他讲述了一小群登山者的故事
he describes their difficult and almost vertical way up
他描述了他们艰难且几乎垂直的上升方式
to the very foot of the last and greatest precipice
到最后也是最大的悬崖脚下
his account tells of how they built a night shelter
他的叙述讲述了他们如何建造夜间避难所
amidst the snow upon a little shelf of rock
在积雪中，在一块小小的岩石架子上
he tells the story with a touch of real dramatic power
他以真正的戏剧力量讲述了这个故事
Nunez had gone from them in the night
努涅斯在夜里离开了他们
They shouted, but there was no reply
他们大喊大叫，但没有回应
and for the rest of that night they slept no more
那天晚上剩下的时间里，他们再也睡不着了
As the morning broke they saw the traces of his fall
天亮时，他们看到了他摔倒的痕迹
It seems impossible he could have uttered a sound
他似乎不可能发出声音
He had slipped eastward
他向东溜走了
towards the unknown side of the mountain
朝向山的未知一侧
far below he had struck a steep slope of snow
在远处，他撞上了陡峭的雪坡
and he must have tumbled all the way down it
他一定是一路跌倒的
in the midst of a snow avalanche
在雪崩中
His track went straight to the edge of a frightful precipice

他的足迹直奔可怕的悬崖边缘
and beyond that everything was hidden
除此之外，一切都被隐藏起来了
Far below, and hazy with distance, they could see trees rising
在远处，在朦胧的远处，他们可以看到树木在上升
out of a narrow, shut-in valley
走出一个狭窄的、封闭的山谷
the lost Country of the Blind
失落的盲人国度
But they did not know it was the Country of the Blind
但他们不知道这是盲人之国
they could not distinguish it from any other narrow valley
他们无法将它与任何其他狭窄的山谷区分开来
Unnerved by this disaster, they abandoned their attempt
他们对这场灾难感到不安，放弃了尝试
and Pointer was called away to the war
指针被召唤去打仗
later he did make another attempt at the mountain
后来，他确实在山上进行了另一次尝试
To this day Parascotopetl lifts an unconquered crest
时至今日，帕拉斯科托佩特尔仍举起了未被征服的顶峰
and Pointer's shelter crumbles unvisited, amidst the snows
Pointer的避难所在雪地中无人问津
And the man who fell survived...
而摔倒的人活了下来......
At the end of the slope he fell a thousand feet
在斜坡的尽头，他跌落了一千英尺
he came down in the midst of a cloud of snow
他在一团雪中下来了
he landed on a snow-slope even steeper than the one

above
他降落在一个比上面更陡峭的雪坡上
Down this slope he was whirled
沿着这个斜坡,他被旋转了
the fall stunned him and he lost consciousness
摔倒使他目瞪口呆,他失去了知觉
but not a bone in his body was broken
但他身上没有一根骨头被折断
finally, he fell down the gentler slopes
最后,他从较缓的斜坡上摔了下来
and at last he laid still
最后他躺着不动了
he was buried amidst a softening heap of the white snow
他被埋葬在一堆软化的白雪中
the snow that had accompanied and saved him
伴随他并拯救他的雪
He came to himself with a dim fancy that he was ill in bed
他朦朦胧胧地回过神来,觉得自己病在床上
then he realized what had happened
然后他意识到发生了什么
with a mountaineer's intelligence he worked himself loose
凭借登山者的智慧,他放松了自己
from the snow he saw the stars
从雪地里,他看到了星星
He rested flat upon his chest
他平躺在胸前
he wondered where he was
他想知道自己在哪里
and he wondered what had happened to him
他想知道他发生了什么事
He explored his limbs to check for damage

他探索了自己的四肢以检查是否有损坏
he discovered that several of his buttons were gone
他发现他的几个纽扣不见了
and his coat was turned over his head
他的外套被翻到头上
His knife had gone from his pocket
他的刀从口袋里掏了出来
and his hat was lost too
他的帽子也丢了
even though he had tied it under his chin
即使他把它绑在下巴下面
He recalled that he had been looking for loose stones
他回忆说,他一直在寻找松散的石头
he wanted to raise his part of the shelter wall
他想抬高他那部分的避难所墙
He realized he must have fallen
他意识到自己一定是摔倒了
and he looked up to see how far he had fallen
他抬起头来,想看看自己跌倒了多远
the cliff was exaggerated by the ghastly light of the rising moon
悬崖被冉冉升起的月亮的可怕光芒夸大了
the fall he had taken was tremendous
他所遭受的跌倒是巨大的
For a while he lay without moving
他躺了一会儿,一动不动
he gazed blankly at the vast, pale cliff
他茫然地凝视着巨大而苍白的悬崖
the mountain towered above him
这座山耸立在他上方
each moment it looked like it kept rising
每时每刻它看起来都在不断上升
rising out of a subsiding tide of darkness
从黑暗的消退浪潮中崛起

Its phantasmal, mysterious beauty held him
它幻影般的神秘之美抓住了他
and then he was seized with sobbing laughter
然后他被抽泣的笑声抓住了
After a great interval of time he became more aware
过了很长一段时间后,他变得更加清醒
he was laying near the lower edge of the snow
他躺在雪的下边缘附近
Below him the slope looked less steep
在他脚下,斜坡看起来不那么陡峭
he saw the dark and broken appearance of rock-strewn turf
他看到了布满岩石的草皮的黑暗和破碎的样子
He struggled to his feet, aching in every joint
他挣扎着站起来,每个关节都疼痛
he got down painfully from the heaped loose snow
他痛苦地从堆积的松散的雪地上下来
and he went downward until he was on the turf
他往下走,直到他躺在草皮上
there he dropped beside a boulder
在那里,他掉在一块巨石旁边
he drank from the flask in his inner pocket
他从内袋里的瓶子里喝了一口
and he instantly fell asleep
他立刻睡着了
He was awakened by the singing of birds
他被鸟儿的歌声吵醒
they were in the trees far below
他们在远处的树上
He sat up and perceived he was on a little alp
他坐了起来,感觉到自己在一个小阿尔卑斯山上
at the foot of a vast precipice
在巨大的悬崖脚下
a precipice that sloped only a little in the gully

沟壑中只有一点点倾斜的悬崖
the path down which he and his snow had come
他和他的雪所走的那条路
against him another wall of rock reared itself against the sky
在他面前，另一堵岩墙向天空升起
The gorge between these precipices ran east and west
这些悬崖之间的峡谷东西向延伸
and it was full of the morning sunlight
它充满了早晨的阳光
the sunlight lit the westward mass of fallen mountain
阳光照亮了西边倒塌的山体
he could see it closed the descending gorge
他可以看到它关闭了下降的峡谷
Below there was a precipice equally steep
下面有一个同样陡峭的悬崖
behind the snow in the gully he found a sort of chimney-cleft
在沟壑的积雪后面，他发现了一个烟囱裂缝
it was dripping with snow-water
它滴着雪水
a desperate man might be able to venture it
一个绝望的人也许可以冒险
He found it easier than it seemed
他发现这比看起来容易
and at last he came to another desolate alp
最后，他来到了另一个荒凉的阿尔卑斯山
there was a rock climb of no particular difficulty
有一次没有特别困难的攀岩
and he reached a steep slope of trees
他走到一个陡峭的树坡上
from here he was able to get his bearings
从这里开始，他能够找到自己的方向
he turned his face up the gorge

他把脸转向峡谷
he saw it opened into green meadows
他看到它被打开成绿色的草地
there he saw quite distinctly the glimmer of some stone huts
在那里,他清楚地看到一些石屋的微光
although the huts looked very strange
虽然小屋看起来很奇怪
even from a distance they didn't look like normal huts
即使从远处看,它们看起来也不像普通的小屋
At times his progress was like clambering along the face of a wall
有时,他的进步就像沿着墙面攀爬一样
and after a time the rising sun ceased to strike along the gorge
过了一会儿,冉冉升起的太阳不再沿着峡谷照射
the voices of the singing birds died away
歌唱的鸟儿的声音消失了
and the air grew cold and dark
空气变得寒冷而黑暗
But the distant valley with its houses got brighter
但远处的山谷及其房屋变得更加明亮
He came to the edge of another cliff
他来到了另一个悬崖的边缘
he was an observant man
他是一个善于观察的人
among the rocks he noted an unfamiliar fern
在岩石中,他注意到一种陌生的蕨类植物
it seemed to clutch out of the crevices with intense green hands
它似乎用强烈的绿色手从缝隙中抓了出来
He picked some of these new plants
他挑选了一些新植物
and he gnawed their stalks

他啃了他们的茎

they gave him strength and energy
他们给了他力量和能量
About midday he came out of the throat of the gorge
大约中午时分，他从峡谷的喉咙里出来了
and he came into the plain of the valley
他来到了山谷的平原上
here he was in the sunlight again
在这里，他又回到了阳光下
He was stiff and weary
他僵硬而疲惫
he sat down in the shadow of a rock
他在岩石的阴影下坐下
he filled up his flask with water from a spring
他用泉水装满了烧瓶
and he drank the spring water
他喝了泉水
he remained where he was for some time
他在原地呆了一段时间
before going to the houses he had decided to rest
在去房子之前，他决定休息一下
They were very strange to his eyes
在他眼里，它们非常奇怪
the more he looked around, the stranger the valley seemed
他越是环顾四周，山谷似乎就越陌生
The greater part of its surface was lush green meadow
其表面的大部分是郁郁葱葱的绿色草地
it was starred with many beautiful flowers
它开满了许多美丽的花朵
extraordinary care had been taken for the irrigation
灌溉工作格外小心
and there was evidence of systematic cropping
并且有系统种植的证据

High up around the valley was a wall
山谷周围高处有一堵墙
there also appeared to be a circumferential water channel
似乎还有一条环形水道
the little trickles of water fed the meadow plants
涓涓细流滋养着草地上的植物
on the higher slopes above this were flocks of llamas
在上方较高的山坡上，有成群的骆驼
they cropped the scanty herbage
他们收割了稀少的草本植物
there were some shelters for the llamas
骆驼有一些避难所
they had been built against the boundary wall
它们建在边界墙上
The irrigation streams ran together into a main channel
灌溉溪流汇入一条主河道
these ran down the centre of the valley
它们沿着山谷的中心流淌
and this was enclosed on either side by a wall chest high
这被一堵胸高的墙围在两边
This gave an urban quality to this secluded place
这为这个僻静的地方赋予了城市品质
a number of paths were paved with black and white stones
许多小路都是用黑白石头铺成的
and the paths had a strange kerb at the side
小路的侧面有一个奇怪的路缘石
this made it seem even more urban
这使它看起来更加城市化
The houses of the central village were not randomly arranged
中心村的房屋不是随意布置的

they stood in a continuous row
他们站成一排
and they were on both sides of the central street
他们在中央大街的两边
here and there the odd walls were pierced by a door
奇怪的墙壁在这里和那里被一扇门刺穿
but there was not a single window to be seen
但是没有一扇窗户可看
They were coloured with extraordinary irregularity
它们的颜色非常不规则
they had been smeared with a sort of plaster
他们被涂上了一种石膏
sometimes it was grey, sometimes drab
有时是灰色的，有时是单调的
sometimes it was slate-coloured
有时它是石板色的
at other times it was dark brown
在其他时候，它是深棕色的
it was the wild plastering that first elicited the word blind
正是这种狂野的抹灰首先引发了"盲人"这个词
"whoever did this must have been as blind as a bat"
"不管是谁干的，一定是像蝙蝠一样瞎了眼"
but also notable was their astonishing cleanness
但同样值得注意的是它们惊人的清洁度
He descended down a steep place
他从一个陡峭的地方下来
and so he came to the wall
于是他来到了墙边
this wall led the water around the valley
这堵墙将水引向山谷周围
and it ended near the bottom of the village
它结束于村庄的底部附近
He could now see a number of men and women

他现在可以看到一些男人和女人

they were resting on piled heaps of grass
他们躺在堆积的草堆上

they seemed to be taking a siesta
他们似乎在午睡

in the remoter part there were a number of children
在较偏远的地方,有许多孩子

and then, nearer to him, there were three men
然后,在他附近,有三个人

they were carrying pails along a little path
他们提着桶沿着一条小路走

the paths ran from the wall towards the houses
小路从墙上一直延伸到房屋

The men were clad in garments of llama cloth
这些人穿着骆驼布的衣服

and their boots and belts were of leather
他们的靴子和腰带是皮革的

and they wore caps of cloth
他们戴着布帽

They followed one another in single file
他们在单个文件中彼此跟随

they yawned as they slowly walked
他们一边打着哈欠,一边慢慢地走着

like men who have been up all night
就像熬夜的男人

Their movement seemed prosperous and respectable
他们的运动似乎繁荣而受人尊敬

Nunez only hesitated for a moment
努涅斯只犹豫了一会儿

and then he came out from behind his rock
然后他从岩石后面出来了

he gave vent to a mighty shout
他发泄了一声有力的呐喊

and his voice echoed round the valley

他的声音在山谷中回荡

The three men stopped and moved their heads
三个人停了下来，动了动脑袋

They seemed to be looking around
他们似乎在环顾四周

They turned their faces this way and that way
他们把脸转过来，转过来，把脸转过来

and Nunez gesticulated wildly
努涅斯疯狂地打着手势

But they did not appear to see him
但他们似乎没有看到他

despite all his waving and gestures
尽管他所有的挥手和手势

eventually they stood themselves towards the mountains
最终，他们向山上站了起来

these were far away to the right
这些在右边很远的地方

and they shouted as if they were answering
他们大喊大叫，好像在回答

Nunez bawled again, and he gestured ineffectually
努涅斯又咆哮了一声，他无能为力地做了个手势

"The fools must be blind," he said
"傻瓜一定是瞎子，"他说

all the shouting and waving didn't help
所有的喊叫和挥手都无济于事

so Nunez crossed the stream by a little bridge
于是努涅斯通过一座小桥过了小溪

he came through a gate in the wall
他穿过墙上的一扇门

and he approached them directly
他直接走近他们

he was sure that they were blind
他确信他们是瞎子

he was sure that this was the Country of the Blind
他确信这是盲人的国家
the country of which the legends told
传说讲述的国家
he had a sense of great adventure
他有一种伟大的冒险精神
The three stood side by side
三人并肩站着
but they did not look at him
但他们没有看他
however, their ears were directed towards him
然而,他们的耳朵对准了他
they judged him by his unfamiliar steps
他们通过他不熟悉的脚步来判断他
They stood close together, like men a little afraid
他们站得很近,像个有点害怕的人
and he could see their eyelids were closed and sunken
他可以看到他们的眼睑紧闭着,凹陷了
as though the very balls beneath had shrunk away
仿佛下面的球已经缩小了
There was an expression near awe on their faces
他们的脸上露出近乎敬畏的表情
"A man," one said to the others
"一个男人,"一个人对其他人说
Nunez hardly recognized the Spanish
努涅斯几乎认不出西班牙人
"A man it is. Or it a spirit"
"这是一个男人。或者它是一种精神"
"he come down from the rocks"
"他从岩石上下来"
Nunez advanced with the confident steps
努涅斯自信地迈着前进的步伐
like a youth who enters upon life
像一个进入生命的青年

All the old stories of the lost valley
失落山谷的所有古老故事
all the stories of the Country of the Blind
盲人之国的所有故事
it all come back to his mind
这一切都回到了他的脑海中
and through his thoughts ran an old proverb
在他的脑海中流淌着一句古老的谚语
"In the Country of the Blind..."
"在瞎子的国度……"
"...the One-Eyed Man is King"
"……独眼人为王"
"In the Country of the Blind the One-Eyed Man is King"
"在瞎子的国度，独眼人是王"
very civilly he gave them greeting
他非常有礼貌地向他们打招呼
He talked to them and used his eyes
他和他们说话，用他的眼睛
"Where does he come from, brother Pedro?" asked one
"他从哪里来，佩德罗兄弟？"一个人问
"from out of the rocks"
"从岩石中走出来"
"I come from over the mountains," said Nunez
"我来自山上，"努涅斯说
"I'm from the country where where men can see"
"我来自男人可以看到的国家"
"I'm from a place near Bogota"
"我来自波哥大附近的一个地方"
"there there are hundreds of thousands of people"
"那里有数十万人"
"the city is so big it goes over the horizon"
"这个城市太大了，它越过了地平线"
"Sight?" muttered Pedro

"视线?"佩德罗咕哝道

"He comes out of the rocks," said the second blind man
"他从岩石里出来了,"第二个瞎子说

The cloth of their coats was curiously fashioned
他们外套的布料造型很奇怪

each patch was of a different sort of stitching
每个补丁都有不同的缝合方式

They startled him by a simultaneous movement towards him
他们同时向他移动,吓了他一跳

each of them had his hand outstretched
他们每个人都伸出了手

He stepped back from the advance of these spread fingers
他从这些张开的手指的前进中退后了一步

"Come hither," said the third blind man
"到这里来,"第三个瞎子说

and he followed Nunez' motion
他听从了努涅斯的动作

he quickly had hold of him
他很快就抓住了他

they held Nunez and felt him over
他们抱着努涅斯,感觉到他过来了

they said no word further until they were done
他们没有再说一句话,直到他们说完

"Careful!" he exclaimed, with a finger in his eye
"小心!"他用手指指着眼睛喊道

they had found a strange organ on him
他们在他身上发现了一个奇怪的器官

"it has fluttering skin"
"它的皮肤会飘动"

"it is very strange indeed"
"这确实很奇怪"

They went over it again

他们又看了一遍

"A strange creature, Correa," said the one called Pedro
"一个奇怪的生物，科雷亚，"那个叫佩德罗的人说

"Feel the coarseness of his hair"
"感受他头发的粗糙"

"it's like a llama's hair"
"这就像骆驼的头发"

"Rough he is as the rocks that begot him," said Correa
"他就像生他的石头一样粗糙，"科雷亚说

and he investigated Nunez's unshaven chin
他调查了努涅斯未刮胡子的下巴

his hands were soft and slightly moist
他的手很柔软，微微湿润

"Perhaps he will grow finer"
"也许他会长得更好"

Nunez tried to free himself from their examination
努涅斯试图从他们的检查中解脱出来

but they had a firm grip on him
但他们牢牢地抓住了他

"Careful," he said again "he speaks"
"小心，"他又说，"他说话"

"we can be sure that he is a man"
"我们可以确定他是一个男人"

"Ugh!" said Pedro, at the roughness of his coat
"呃！"佩德罗说，看着他粗糙的外套

"And you have come into the world?" asked Pedro
"你来到这个世界了吗？"佩德罗问

"I come from the world out there"
"我来自外面的世界"

"I come from over mountains and glaciers"
"我来自高山和冰川"

"it is half-way to the sun"
"这是太阳的一半"

"Out of the great, big world that goes down"

"走出那个伟大的、大的世界"
"twelve days' journey to the sea"
"十二天的海上之旅"
They scarcely seemed to heed him
他们似乎几乎不理会他
"Our fathers have told us of such things"
"我们的祖先已经告诉我们这些事情"
"men may be made by the forces of Nature," said Correa
"人可能是由自然的力量创造的，"科雷亚说
"Let us lead him to the elders," said Pedro
"让我们带他去见长老，"佩德罗说
"Shout first," said Correa
"先喊，"科雷亚说
"the children might be afraid"
"孩子们可能会害怕"
"This is a marvellous occasion"
"这是一个了不起的时刻"
So they shouted to the others
于是他们向其他人喊道
Pedro took Nunez by the hand
佩德罗拉着努涅斯的手
and he lead him to the houses
他把他带到房子里
He drew his hand away
他把手抽开
"I can see," he said
"我能看到，"他说
"to see?" said Correa
"看看吗？"科雷亚说
"Yes, I can see with my eyes," said Nunez
"是的，我可以用眼睛看到，"努涅斯说
and he turned towards him
他转向他

but he stumbled against Pedro's pail
但他绊倒了佩德罗的桶
"His senses are still imperfect," said the third blind man
"他的感官还不完美，"第三个盲人说
"He stumbles, and talks unmeaning words"
"他跌跌撞撞，说着毫无意义的话"
"Lead him by the hand"
"牵着他的手"
"As you will" said Nunez
"如你所愿，"努涅斯说
and he was led along
他被领着走
but he had to laugh at the situation
但他不得不嘲笑这种情况
it seemed they knew nothing of sight
他们似乎对视力一无所知
"I will teach them soon enough," he thought to himself
"我很快就会教他们的，"他心想
He heard people shouting
他听到有人大喊大叫
and he saw a number of figures gathering together
他看到一些人聚集在一起
he saw them in the middle roadway of the village
他在村子的中间巷道里看到了他们
all of it taxed his nerve and patience
所有这些都消耗了他的神经和耐心
there were more than he had anticipated
比他预想的要多
this was the first encounter with the population
这是第一次与民众相遇
the people from the Country of the Blind
来自盲人之国的人
The place seemed larger as he drew near to it

当他靠近它时，这个地方似乎更大了
and the smeared plasterings became even queerer
涂抹的石膏变得更加奇怪
a crowd of children and men and women came around him
一群孩子和男人和女人围着他
they all tried to hold on to him
他们都试图抓住他
they touched him with their soft and sensitive hands
他们用柔软而敏感的手抚摸着他
not surprisingly, they smelled at him too
毫不奇怪，他们也闻到了他的味道
and they listened at every word he spoke
他们听他说的每一句话
some of the women and girls had quite sweet faces
一些妇女和女孩的脸上写着相当甜美的面孔
even though their eyes were shut and sunken
即使他们的眼睛是闭着的，凹陷的
he thought this would make his stay more pleasant
他认为这会让他的逗留更加愉快
However, some of the maidens and children kept aloof
然而，一些少女和孩子保持冷漠
they seemed to be afraid of him
他们似乎害怕他
his voice seemed coarse and rude beside their softer notes
他的声音在他们柔和的音符旁边显得粗糙而粗鲁
it is reasonable to say the crowd mobbed him
可以说人群围攻他是合理的
but his three guides kept close to him
但他的三个向导一直紧紧地贴在他身边
they had taken some pride and ownership in him
他们为他感到骄傲和所有权
again and again they said, "A wild man out of the

rocks"
他们一遍又一遍地说,"一个从岩石里出来的野人"
"Bogota," he said, "Over the mountain crests"
"波哥大,"他说,"越过山峰"
"A wild man using wild words," said Pedro
"一个用狂野语言的野人,"佩德罗说
"Did you hear that, Bogota?"
"你听到了吗,波哥大?"
"His mind has hardly formed yet"
"他的思想还没有形成"
"He has only the beginnings of speech"
"他只有言语的开端"
A little boy nipped his hand
一个小男孩咬住了他的手
"Bogota!" he said mockingly
"波哥大!"他嘲弄地说
"Aye! A city to your village"
"哎呀!一个城市到你的村庄"
"I come from the great world"
"我来自伟大的世界"
"the world where men have eyes and see"
"男人有眼睛和看到的世界"
"His name's Bogota," they said
"他的名字叫波哥大,"他们说
"He stumbled," said Correa
"他跌跌撞撞,"科雷亚说
"he stumbled twice as we came hither"
"当我们来到这里时,他绊倒了两次"
"bring him in to the elders"
"把他带到长老那里去"
And they thrust him through a doorway
他们把他推到门口
he found himself in a room as black as pitch
他发现自己身处一个漆黑如沥青的房间里

but slowly his eyes adjusted to the darkness
但慢慢地,他的眼睛适应了黑暗
at the far end a fire faintly glowed
在远端,一团火微弱地发光
The crowd closed in behind him
人群在他身后合拢
and they shut out any light that could have come from outside
他们关闭了任何可能来自外面的光线
before he could stop himself he had fallen
还没等他停下来,他就摔倒了
he fell right into the lap of a seated man
他正好倒在一个坐着的人的腿上
and his arm struck the face of someone else
他的胳膊撞到了别人的脸上
he felt the soft impact of features
他感受到了功能的柔和冲击
and he heard a cry of anger
他听见一声愤怒的呼喊
for a moment he struggled against a number of hands
有那么一会儿,他与几只手搏斗
all of them were clutching him
他们都紧紧抓住他
but it was a one-sided fight
但这是一场一边倒的战斗
An inkling of the situation came to him
他恍然大悟
and he decided to lay quiet
他决定安静下来
"I fell down," he said
"我摔倒了,"他说
"I couldn't see in this pitchy darkness"
"在这漆黑的黑暗中,我看不见"
There was a pause at what he had said

他说的话停顿了一下

he felt unseen persons trying to understand his words
他感觉到看不见的人试图理解他的话

Then he heard the voice of Correa
然后他听到了科雷亚的声音

"He is but newly formed"
"他只是新成立的"

"He stumbles as he walks"
"他走路时跌跌撞撞"

"and his speech mingles words that mean nothing"
"他的讲话混合了毫无意义的词语"

Others also said things about him
其他人也说了他的事情

they all confirmed they could not perfectly understand him
他们都证实他们无法完全理解他

"May I sit up?" he asked during a pause
"我可以坐起来吗?"他停顿了一下问道

"I will not struggle against you again"
"我不会再和你作斗争了"

the elders consulted, and let him rise
长老们商量了一下,就让他起来

The voice of an older man began to question him
一个年长的男人的声音开始质问他

again, Nunez found himself trying to explain the world
再一次,努涅斯发现自己试图解释世界

the great world out of which he had fallen
他从中坠落的伟大世界

he told them of the sky and mountains
他告诉他们天空和山脉

and he tried to convey other such marvels
他试图传达其他这样的奇迹

but the elders sat in darkness

但长老们却坐在黑暗中
and they did not know of the Country of the Blind
他们不知道瞎子之国
if only he could show these elders
要是他能给这些长辈看就好了
but they believed and understood nothing
但他们什么都不相信，什么也不明白
whatever he told them created confusion
无论他告诉他们是否都会引起混乱
it was all quite outside his expectations
这一切都出乎他的意料
They did not understand many of his words
他们听不懂他的许多话
For generations these people had been blind
几代人以来，这些人都是盲人
and they had been cut off from all the seeing world
他们被切断了与所有看得见的世界的联系
the names for all the things of sight had faded and changed
所有视觉事物的名称都消失了，改变了
the story of the outer world had become a story
外面世界的故事变成了一个故事
his world was just something people told their children
他的世界只是人们告诉孩子的东西
and they had ceased to concern themselves with it
他们已经不再关心它了
the only thing of interest was inside the rocky slopes
唯一有趣的是在岩石斜坡内
they lived only in their circling wall
他们只住在他们盘旋的墙上
Blind men of genius had arisen among them
在他们中间出现了天才的盲人
they had questioned the old believes and traditions

他们质疑旧的信仰和传统
and they had dismissed all these things as idle fancies
他们把所有这些事情都当作无聊的幻想
they replaced them with new and saner explanations
他们用新的、更理智的解释取而代之
Much of their imagination had shrivelled with their eyes
他们的大部分想象力都因眼睛而萎缩
their ears and finger-tips had gotten ever more sensitive
他们的耳朵和指尖变得越来越敏感
and with these they had made themselves new imaginations
有了这些,他们为自己创造了新的想象力
Slowly Nunez realised the situation he was in
慢慢地,努涅斯意识到了他所处的境地
he could not expect any reverence for his origin
他不能指望对他的出身有任何崇敬
his gifts were not as useful as he thought
他的天赋并不像他想象的那么有用
explaining sight was not going to be easy
解释视力并不容易
his attempts had been quite incoherent
他的尝试非常不连贯
he was deflated from his initial excitement
他从最初的兴奋中泄气了
and he subsided into listening to their instruction
于是他就静下心来听他们的吩咐
the eldest of the blind men explained to him life
最年长的瞎子向他解释生活
he explained to him philosophy and religion
他向他解释了哲学和宗教
he described the origins of the world
他描述了世界的起源

(by this of course he meant the valley)
（当然，他指的是山谷）

first it had been an empty hollow in the rocks
起初，它是岩石中的一个空洞

first came inanimate things without the gift of touch
首先是没有触觉天赋的无生命事物

then came llamas and other creatures of little sense
然后是骆驼和其他毫无意义的生物

when all had been put in place, men came
当一切都就位时，人们来了

and finally angels came to the world
最后，天使来到了这个世界

one could hear the angels singing and making fluttering sounds
人们可以听到天使在唱歌，发出飘动的声音

but it was impossible to touch them
但不可能碰到它们

this explanation first puzzled Nunez greatly
这个解释首先让努涅斯感到非常困惑

but then he thought of the birds
但后来他想到了鸟儿

He went on to tell Nunez how time had been divided
他接着告诉努涅斯时间是如何分配的

there was the warm time and the cold time
有温暖的时光，也有寒冷的时光

of course these are the blind equivalents of day and night
当然，这些都是白天和黑夜的盲目等价物

he told how it was good to sleep in the warm
他讲述了在温暖的环境中睡觉是多么好

he explained how it was better to work during the cold
他解释了在寒冷中工作如何更好

normally the whole town of the blind would now have been asleep

正常情况下，整个瞎子镇现在都睡着了
but this special event kept them up
但这次特殊事件让他们坚持了下来
He said Nunez must have been specially created to learn
他说努涅斯一定是专门为学习而创造的
and he was there to serve the wisdom they had acquired
他在那里服侍他们所获得的智慧
his mental incoherency was ignored, for the time being
他的精神不连贯暂时被忽视了
and he was forgiven for his stumbling behaviour
他的磕磕绊绊的行为被原谅了
he was told to have courage in this world
他被告知在这个世界上要有勇气
and he was told to do his best to learn
他被告知要尽最大努力学习
all the people in the doorway murmured encouragingly
门口所有的人都鼓励地窃窃私语
He said the night was far gone
他说那一夜已经过去了
(the blind call their day night)
（瞎子称他们白天为黑夜）
so he encouraged everyone to go back to sleep
所以他鼓励大家回去睡觉
He asked Nunez if he knew how to sleep
他问努涅斯是否知道如何睡觉
Nunez said he did know how to sleep
努涅斯说他确实知道如何睡觉
but that before sleep he wanted food
但是在睡觉之前，他想吃东西
They brought him some of their food
他们给他带来了一些食物

llama's milk in a bowl and rough salted bread
骆驼的牛奶在碗里和粗糙的咸面包
and they led him into a lonely place
他们把他带到一个寂寞的地方
so that he could eat out of their hearing
这样他就可以吃掉他们的耳朵
afterwards he was allowed to slumber
之后，他被允许睡觉
until the chill of the mountain evening roused them
直到山间傍晚的寒意将他们唤醒
and then they would begin their day again
然后他们又开始新的一天
But Nunez slumbered not at all
但努涅斯根本没有睡着
Instead, he sat up in the place where they had left him
相反，他在他们离开他的地方坐了起来
he rested his limbs, still sore from the fall
他休息了一下四肢，仍然因跌倒而酸痛
and he turned everything over and over in his mind
他在脑海里翻来覆去
the unanticipated circumstances of his arrival
他到来的意想不到的情况
Every now and then he laughed
他时不时地笑
sometimes with amusement, and sometimes with indignation
有时是逗乐，有时是愤慨
"Unformed mind!" he said, "Got no senses yet!"
"未成形的头脑！"他说，"还没有知觉！
"little do they know what they're saying!"
"他们几乎不知道自己在说什么！"
"they've been insulting their Heaven-sent King and master"
"他们一直在侮辱他们的天赐之王和主人"

"I see I must bring them to reason"
"我明白了,我必须让他们讲道理"
"Let me think about this..."
"让我考虑一下......"
He was still thinking when the sun set
太阳落山时,他还在思考
Nunez had an eye for all beautiful things
努涅斯对所有美丽的事物都有眼光
he saw the glow upon the snow-fields and glaciers
他看到了雪原和冰川上的光芒
on the mountains that rose about the valley on every side
在山谷四面八方耸立的山上
it was the most beautiful thing he had ever seen
这是他见过的最美丽的东西
His eyes went over the inaccessible glory to the village
他的目光扫过村庄难以企及的荣耀
he looked over irrigated fields sinking into the twilight
他望着沉入暮色的灌溉田地
suddenly a wave of emotion hit him
突然,一股情绪向他袭来
he thanked God from the bottom of his heart
他从心底里感谢上帝
"thank you for the power of sight you have given me"
"谢谢你给我的视力"
He heard a voice calling to him
他听到一个声音在呼唤他
it was coming from the village
它来自村庄
"ahoi-hoi, Bogota! Come hither!"
"啊,波哥大!到这里来!"
At that he stood up, smiling
听到这话,他站了起来,微笑着

He would show these people once and for all!
他会一劳永逸地向这些人展示!

"they will learn what sight can do for a man!"
"他们将了解视力可以为男人做些什么!"

"I shall make them seek me"
"我要叫他们找我"

"but they shall not be able to find me"
"但他们找不到我"

"You move not, Bogota," said the voice
"你别动,波哥大,"那个声音说

at this he laughed, without making a noise
听到这话,他笑了,没有发出任何声音

he made two stealthy steps from the path
他悄悄地从小路上走了两步

"Trample not on the grass, Bogota"
"不要踩在草地上,波哥大"

"wondering off the path is not allowed"
"不允许偏离路径"

Nunez had scarcely heard the sound he made himself
努涅斯几乎听不到他自己发出的声音

He stopped where he was, amazed
他停在原地,惊讶地

the owner of the voice came running up the path
声音的主人沿着小路跑了过来

and he stepped back into the pathway
然后他又回到了小路上

"Here I am," he said
"我在这里,"他说

the blind man was not impressed with Nunez's antics
盲人对努涅斯的滑稽动作没有留下深刻的印象

"Why did you not come when I called you?"
"我叫你的时候你怎么还没来?"

"Must you be led like a child?"
"你必须像个孩子一样被牵着走吗?"

"Cannot you hear the path as you walk?"
"你走的时候听不到路吗？"

Nunez laughed at the ridiculous questions
努涅斯嘲笑了这些荒谬的问题

"I can see it," he said
"我能看到它，"他说

the blind man paused for a moment
瞎子停顿了一会儿

"There is no such word as see"
"没有看这样的词"

"Cease this folly and follow the sound of my feet"
"停止这种愚蠢，听从我的脚步声"

Nunez followed the blind man, a little annoyed
努涅斯跟在瞎子身后，有点恼火

"My time will come," he said to himself
"我的时代会到来的，"他对自己说

"You'll learn," the blind man answered
"你会学会的，"瞎子回答

"There is much to learn in the world"
"世界上有很多东西要学"

"Has no one told you?" asked Nunez
"没人告诉你吗？"努涅斯问

"In the Country of the Blind the One-Eyed Man is King"
"在瞎子的国度，独眼人是王"

"What is blind?" asked the blind man, over his shoulder
"什么是瞎子？"瞎子在他肩膀上问道

by now four days had passed
到现在已经过去了四天

even on the fifth day nothing had changed
即使在第五天，一切都没有改变

the King of the Blind was still incognito
瞎子之王仍然隐姓埋名

he was still a clumsy and useless stranger among his subjects
在他的臣民中,他仍然是一个笨拙而无用的陌生人
he found it all much more difficult than he thought
他发现这一切比他想象的要困难得多
how could he proclaim himself king to these blind people??
他怎么能向这些瞎子宣布自己为王??
he was left to meditated his coup d'etat
他被留下来沉思他的政变
in the meantime he did what he was told
与此同时,他按照他的吩咐做了
he learnt the manners and customs of the Country of the Blind
他学会了盲人之国的礼仪和习俗
working at night he found particularly irksome
晚上工作,他觉得特别烦人
this was going to be the first thing he changed
这将是他改变的第一件事
They led a simple and laborious life
他们过着简单而艰苦的生活
but they had all the elements of virtue and happiness
但他们拥有美德和幸福的所有元素
They toiled, but not oppressively
他们辛勤工作,但不是压迫性的
they had food and clothing sufficient for their needs
他们有足够满足他们需要的食物和衣服
they had days and seasons of rest
他们有几天和几个季节的休息
they enjoyed music and singing
他们喜欢音乐和唱歌
there was love among them
他们之间有爱
and there were little children

还有小孩子
It was marvellous to see their confidence and precision
看到他们的信心和精确度真是太棒了
they went about their ordered world efficiently
他们有效地度过了他们有序的世界
Everything had been made to fit their needs
一切都是为了满足他们的需求而制作的
each paths had a constant angle to the other
每条路径与另一条路径的角度恒定
each kerb was distinguished by a special notch
每个路缘都有一个特殊的缺口
all obstacles and irregularities had been cleared away
所有障碍和违规行为都已清除
all their methods arose naturally from their special needs
他们所有的方法都是从他们的特殊需求中自然而然产生的
and their procedures made sense to their abilities
他们的程序对他们的能力有意义
their senses had become marvellously acute
他们的感官变得非常敏锐
they could hear and judge the slightest gesture
他们能听到并判断最轻微的手势
even if the man was a dozen paces away
即使那个人离他只有十几步远
they could hear the very beating of his heart
他们能听到他心脏的跳动
Intonation and touch had long replaced expression and gesture
语调和触觉早已取代了表情和手势
they were handy with the hoe and spade
他们用锄头和铁锹很方便
and they moved as free and confident as any gardener
他们像任何园丁一样自由和自信地移动
Their sense of smell was extraordinarily fine

他们的嗅觉非常好
they could distinguish individual differences as quickly as a dog can
它们可以像狗一样快速区分个体差异
and they went about the tending of llamas with ease and confidence
他们轻松自信地照料骆驼
a day came Nunez sought to assert himself
有一天,努涅斯试图维护自己
but he quickly realized his underestimation
但他很快意识到自己被低估了
and he learned how confident their movements could be
他了解到他们的动作是多么自信
he rebelled only after he had tried persuasion
他只是在尝试说服之后才反抗
on several occasions he had tried to tell them of sight
有好几次,他试图告诉他们视力
"Look you here, you people," he said
"看你们这里,你们这些人,"他说
"There are things you people do not understand in me"
"你们这些人在我身上有些不明白的东西"
Once or twice one or two of them listened to him
有一两次,他们中的一两个人听了他的话
they sat with their faces downcast
他们垂头丧气地坐着
their ears were turned intelligently towards him
他们的耳朵聪明地转向他
and he did his best to tell them what it was to see
他尽力告诉他们要看什么
Among his hearers was a girl
他的听众中有一个女孩
her eyelids were less red and sunken
她的眼睑不那么红了,也不那么凹陷了

one could almost imagine she was hiding eyes
人们几乎可以想象她隐藏着眼睛
he especially hoped to persuade her
他特别希望能说服她
He spoke of the beauties of sight
他谈到了视觉的美丽
he spoke of watching the mountains
他谈到看山
he told them of the sky and the sunrise
他告诉他们天空和日出
and they heard him with amused incredulity
他们听他说话时感到好笑
but that eventually became condemnatory
但这最终变成了谴责
They told him there were no mountains at all
他们告诉他根本没有山
they told him only the llamas go to the rocks
他们告诉他，只有骆驼才会去岩石上
they graze their grass there at the edge
他们在边缘吃草
and that is the end of the world
这就是世界末日
from there the roof rises over the universe
从那里，屋顶在宇宙上空升起
only the dew and the avalanches fell from there
只有露水和雪崩从那里掉下来
he maintained stoutly the world had neither end nor roof
他坚定地认为，世界既没有尽头，也没有屋顶
everything they thought about the world was wrong, he told them
他告诉他们，他们对这个世界的看法都是错误的
but they said his thoughts were wicked
但他们说他的想法是邪恶的

his descriptions of sky and clouds and stars were hideous to them
他对天空、云彩和星星的描述对他们来说是可怕的
a terrible blankness in the place of the smooth roof of the world
在世界光滑的屋顶上，一片可怕的空白
it was an article of faith with them
这是他们信条
they believed the cavern roof was exquisitely smooth to the touch
他们认为洞穴顶部摸起来非常光滑
he saw that in some manner he shocked them
他看到他以某种方式震惊了他们
and he gave up that aspect of the matter altogether
他完全放弃了这件事的那一面
instead, he tried to show them the practical value of sight
相反，他试图向他们展示视觉的实用价值
One morning he saw Pedro on path Seventeen
一天早上，他在十七号小路上看到佩德罗
he was coming towards the central houses
他正向中央的房子走来
but he was still too far away for hearing or scent
但他仍然离得太远，听不到，闻不到气味
"In a little while," he prophesied, "Pedro will be here"
"过一会儿，"他预言道，"佩德罗会在这里
An old man remarked that Pedro had no business on path Seventeen
一位老人说，佩德罗在十七号路上没有生意
and then, as if in confirmation, Pedro changed paths
然后，仿佛在确认，佩德罗改变了道路
with nimble paces he went towards the outer wall
他迈着敏捷的步伐向外墙走去
They mocked Nunez when Pedro did not arrive

当佩德罗没有到来时,他们嘲笑努涅斯
he tried to clear his character by asking Pedro
他试图通过询问佩德罗来清除他的性格
but Pedro denied the allegations
但佩德罗否认了这些指控
and afterwards he was hostile to him
后来他对他怀有敌意
Then he convinced them to let him go
然后他说服他们放了他
"let me go up the sloping meadows to the wall"
"让我爬上倾斜的草地到墙上"
"let me take with me one willing individual"
"让我带一个愿意的人"
"I will describe all that is happening among the houses"
"我将描述房屋之间发生的一切"
He noted certain goings and comings
他注意到某些来来往往
but these things were not important to these people
但这些东西对这些人来说并不重要
they cared for what happened inside the windowless houses
他们关心没有窗户的房子里发生的事情
of those things he could neither see, nor tell
那些他既看不见也说不出来的事情
his attempt had failed again
他的尝试再次失败了
they could not repress their ridicule
他们无法抑制自己的嘲笑
and finally Nunez resorted to force
最后努涅斯诉诸武力
He thought of seizing a spade
他想到了抓住一把铁锹
he could smite one or two of them to earth

他可以把其中的一两个人打倒在地
in fair combat he could show the advantage of eyes
在公平的战斗中,他可以展示眼睛的优势
He went so far with that resolution as to seize his spade
他下定决心走得太远,以至于抓住了铁锹
but then he discovered a new thing about himself
但后来他发现了一件关于自己的新事情
it was impossible for him to hit a blind man in cold blood
他不可能冷血地打一个瞎子
holding the spade, he hesitated for a moment
拿着铁锹,他犹豫了一会儿
all of them had become aware that he had snatched up the spade
他们都意识到他抢走了铁锹
They stood alert, with their heads on one side
他们警觉地站着,头偏向一边
they cautiously bent their ears towards him
他们小心翼翼地向他竖起耳朵
and they waited for what he would do next
他们等着他接下来会做什么
"Put that spade down," said one
"把那把铁锹放下,"一个人说
and he felt a sort of helpless horror
他感到一种无助的恐惧
he could not come to their obedience
他不能顺服他们
he thrust one backwards against a house wall
他把一个人向后推到房子的墙上
and he fled past him, and out of the village
他从他身边逃过,逃出了村子
he went over one of their meadows
他走过他们的一片草地

but of course he trampled grass behind him
但他当然踩踏了他身后的草

he sat down by the side of one of their ways
他在他们其中一条路的旁边坐下

he felt something of the buoyancy in him
他感觉到他身上有某种浮力

all men feel it in the beginning of a fight
所有男人在战斗开始时都会感觉到这一点

but he felt more perplexity than anything
但他感到比任何事情都更困惑

he began to realise something else about himself
他开始意识到自己的其他事情

you cannot fight happily with creatures of a different mental basis
你不能与具有不同精神基础的生物愉快地战斗

Far away he saw a number of men carrying spades and sticks
在很远的地方，他看到一些人拿着铁锹和棍棒

they were coming out of the streets and houses
他们从街道和房屋中走出来

together they made a line across the paths
他们一起在小路上划了一条线

and they line was coming towards him
他们排成一列向他走来

They advanced slowly, speaking frequently to one another
他们缓慢地前进，经常互相交谈

again and again they stopped and sniff the air
他们一次又一次地停下来嗅空气

The first time they did this Nunez laughed
他们第一次这样做时，努涅斯笑了

But afterwards he did not laugh
但后来他没有笑

One found his trail in the meadow grass

一个人在草地上发现了自己的踪迹
he came stooping and feeling his way along it
他弯下腰，摸索着走着
For five minutes he watched the slow extension of the line
在五分钟的时间里，他看着队伍的缓慢延伸
his vague disposition to do something forthwith became frantic
他模糊地想立即做点什么，变得疯狂起来
He stood up and paced towards the wall
他站起身来，踱步向墙边
he turned, and went back a little way
他转过身，往回走了一段路
they all stood in a crescent, still and listening
他们都站在月牙形，静静地听着
He also stood still, gripping his spade
他也站着不动，握着铁锹
Should he attack them?
他应该攻击他们吗？
The pulse in his ears ran into a rhythm:
他耳边的脉搏有节奏：
"In the Country of the Blind the One-Eyed Man is King"
"在瞎子的国度，独眼人是王"
"In the Country of the Blind the One-Eyed Man is King"
"在瞎子的国度，独眼人是王"
"In the Country of the Blind the One-Eyed Man is King"
"在瞎子的国度，独眼人是王"
He looked back at the high and unclimbable wall
他回头看了看那堵高高的、无法攀登的墙
and he looked at the approaching line of seekers
他看着正在逼近的寻道者队伍

others were now coming out of the street of houses too
其他人现在也从房屋街上出来了

"Bogota!" called one, "Where are you?"
"波哥大！"一个人叫道，"你在哪里？"

He gripped his spade even tighter
他把铁锹握得更紧了

and he went down the meadow towards the place of habitations
他沿着草地向居住地走去

where he moved they converged upon him
他走到哪里，他们就聚集在他身上

"I'll hit them if they touch me," he swore
"如果他们碰我，我会打他们，"他发誓

"by Heaven, I will. I'll hit them"
"靠天，我会的。我会打他们"

He called aloud, "Look here you people"
他大声喊道："看你们这些人"

"I'm going to do what I like in this valley!"
"我要在这个山谷里做我喜欢做的事！"

"Do you hear? I'm going to do what I like"
"你听到了吗？我要做我喜欢做的事"

"and I will go where I like"
"我会去我喜欢的地方"

They were moving in upon him quickly
他们很快就向他走来

they were groping at everything, yet moving rapidly
他们摸索着一切，但行动迅速

It was like playing blind man's bluff
这就像在玩瞎子的虚张声势

but everyone was blindfolded except one
但除了一个人之外，每个人都被蒙住了眼睛

"Get hold of him!" cried one
"抓住他！"一个人喊道

He realized a group of men had surrounded him

他意识到一群人包围了他
suddenly he felt he must be active and resolute
突然间，他觉得自己必须积极而果断
"You people don't understand," he cried
"你们不明白，"他喊道
his voice was meant to be great and resolute
他的声音本来就是伟大而坚定的
but his voice broke and carried no power
但他的声音破碎了，没有力量
"You are all blind and I can see"
"你们都是瞎子，我看得见"
"Leave me alone!" he tried to command
"别管我！"他试图命令道
"Bogota! Put down that spade and come off the grass!"
"波哥大！放下那把铁锹，从草地上下来！
the order was grotesque in its familiarity
这个命令在熟悉中是怪诞的
and it produced a gust of anger in him
这在他心中产生了一阵愤怒
"I'll hurt you," he said, sobbing with emotion
"我会伤害你的，"他说，情绪激动地抽泣着
"By Heaven, I'll hurt you! Leave me alone!"
"老天爷，我会伤害你的！别管我！
He began to run without knowing where to run
他开始跑，不知道该跑到哪里去
He ran away from the nearest blind man
他逃离了最近的盲人
because it was a horror to hit him
因为打他真是太可怕了
He made a dash to escape from their closing ranks
他冲向逃离了他们的封闭队伍
in one place the gap was a little wider
在一个地方，差距有点大
the men on the sides quickly perceived what was

happening
两边的人很快就察觉到了发生了什么
they quickly rushed in to close the gap
他们迅速冲进去缩小差距
He sprang forward, and saw he would be caught
他向前跳去，看到自己会被抓住
and whoosh! the spade had struck
嗖！铁锹击中了
He felt the soft thud of hand and arm
他感觉到手和胳膊发出的轻柔砰砰声
and the man was down with a yell of pain
那人痛苦地大叫着倒下了
and he was through the gap
他穿过了缺口
he was close to the street of houses again
他又靠近了房屋的街道
the blind men were whirling their spades and stakes
瞎子们正在旋转他们的铁锹和木桩
and they were running with a new swiftness
他们以新的速度奔跑
He heard steps behind him just in time
他及时听到身后的脚步声
a tall man was rushing towards him
一个高个子男人正向他冲来
he was swiping his spade at the sound of him
听到他的声音，他正在挥舞铁锹
Nunez lost his nerve this time
努涅斯这次失去了勇气
he could not hit another blind man
他不能打另一个瞎子
he hurled his spade next to his antagonist
他把铁锹扔到对手旁边
the tall man whirled about from where he heard the noise

高个子男人从他听到噪音的地方转过身来
and Nunez fled, yelling as he dodged another
努涅斯逃跑了，一边躲闪一边大喊大叫
He was panic-stricken by this point
此时，他惊慌失措
almost blindly, he ran furiously to and fro
他几乎是盲目的，疯狂地跑来跑去
he dodged when there was no need to dodge
当没有必要躲避时，他躲开了
in his anxiety he tried to see every side of him at once
在焦虑中，他试图同时看到他的每一面
for a moment he had fallen down
有那么一会儿，他倒下了
of course the followers heard his fall
当然，追随者听到了他的堕落
he caught a glimpse of something in the circumferential wall
他瞥见了围墙上有什么东西
a little gap between the wall
墙体之间的一点缝隙
he set off in a wild rush for it
他疯狂地冲向它
he had stumbled across the bridge
他跌跌撞撞地过了桥
and he clambered a little along the rocks
他沿着岩石爬了一点
a surprised young llama went leaping out of sight
一只惊讶的小骆驼从视线中跳了出来
and then he lay down, sobbing for breath
然后他躺下，抽泣着喘气
And so his coup d'etat came to an end
因此，他的政变结束了
He stayed outside the wall of the valley of the blind
他呆在瞎子谷的墙外

for two nights and days he was without food or shelter
他昼夜两夜没有食物，也没有住所
and he meditated upon the unexpected
他沉思着意想不到的事情
During these meditations he repeated his motto frequently
在这些冥想中，他经常重复他的座右铭
"In the Country of the Blind the One-Eyed Man is King"
"在瞎子的国度，独眼人是王"
He thought chiefly of ways of conquering these people
他主要考虑的是征服这些人的方法
and it grew clear that no practicable way was possible
很明显，没有可行的方法
He had brought no weapons with him
他没有带武器
and now it would be hard to get any
现在很难得到任何东西
his civilized manner had not left him
他的文明举止并没有离开他
there was no way he could assassinate a blind man
他不可能刺杀一个瞎子
Of course, if he did that, he could dictate the terms
当然，如果他这样做了，他可以决定条款
he could threaten them with further assassinations
他可以用进一步的暗杀来威胁他们
But, sooner or later he must sleep!
但是，他迟早要睡觉！
He tried to find food among the pine trees
他试图在松树中寻找食物
at night the frost fell over the valley
到了晚上，霜冻笼罩着山谷
to be comfortable he slept under pine boughs
为了舒适，他睡在松树枝下

he thought about catching a llama, if he could
如果可以的话，他想抓一只骆驼
perhaps he could hammer it with a stone
也许他可以用石头敲打它
and then he could eat some of it
然后他可以吃一些
But the llamas had doubt of him
但是骆驼们对他产生了怀疑
they regarded him with distrustful brown eyes
他们用不信任的棕色眼睛看着他
and they spat at him when he came near
当他靠近时，他们向他吐口水
Fear came on him the second day
第二天，恐惧降临在他身上
he was taken by fits of shivering
他被一阵颤抖带走了
Finally he crawled back down the wall
最后，他爬下了墙
and he went back into the Country of the Blind
然后他回到了瞎子的国度
he shouted until two blind men came out to the gate
他大喊大叫，直到两个瞎子走到门口
and he talked to him, negotiating his terms
他和他谈了谈，谈判他的条件
"I had gone mad," he said
"我疯了，"他说
"But I was only newly made"
"但我只是新造的"
They said that was better
他们说这样更好
He told them he was wiser now
他告诉他们，他现在更聪明了
and he repented of all he had done
他为自己所做的一切忏悔

Then he wept without reserve
然后他毫无保留地哭了起来
because he was very weak and ill now
因为他现在非常虚弱和生病
they took that as a favourable sign
他们认为这是一个有利的迹象
They asked him if he still thought he could see
他们问他是否还认为他能看到
"No," he said, "That was folly"
"不，"他说，"那是愚蠢的。
"The word means nothing, less than nothing!"
"这个词没有意义，比什么都没有还少！"
They asked him what was overhead
他们问他头顶上有什么
"About ten times ten the height of a man"
"大约是男人身高的十乘以十"
"there is a roof above the world of rock"
"岩石世界之上有一个屋顶"
"it is very, very smooth"
"非常非常顺利"
"So smooth, so beautifully smooth"
"如此光滑，如此美丽光滑"
He burst again into hysterical tears
他再次歇斯底里地流下了眼泪
"Before you ask me any more, give me some food"
"在你再问我之前，先给我一些食物"
"or else I shall die!"
"不然我就死了！"
He expected dire punishments
他预料到会受到可怕的惩罚
but these blind people were capable of toleration
但这些盲人是可以容忍的
his rebellion was just more proof of his idiocy
他的叛逆只是他愚蠢的更多证明

they hardly needed more evidence for his inferiority
他们几乎不需要更多的证据来证明他的自卑

as a punishment he was whipped some
作为惩罚，他被鞭打了一些

and they appointed him to do the heaviest work
他们任命他做最繁重的工作

Nunez could see no other way of surviving
努涅斯看不到其他生存方式

so he submissively did what he was told
所以他顺从地按照他的吩咐去做

he was ill for some days
他病了好几天

and they nursed him kindly
他们亲切地照顾他

that refined his submission
这完善了他的提交

but they insisted on him lying in the dark
但他们坚持让他躺在黑暗中

that was a great misery to him
这对他来说是一个巨大的痛苦

blind philosophers came and talked to him
盲人哲学家来和他交谈

they spoke of the wicked levity of his mind
他们说他心中邪恶的轻浮

and they retold the story of creation
他们重述了创造的故事

they explained further how the world was structured
他們進一步解释了世界是如何结構的

and soon Nunez had doubts about what he thought he knew
很快，努涅斯就怀疑他自以为知道的东西

perhaps he really was the victim of hallucination
也许他真的是幻觉的受害者

and so Nunez became a citizen of the Country of the

Blind
因此,努涅斯成为了盲人之国的公民
and these people ceased to be a generalised people
这些人不再是广义的民族
they became individualities to him
他们成为他的个性
and they grew familiar to him
他们对他来说越来越熟悉
the world beyond the mountains slowly faded
山外的世界慢慢消失了
more and more it became remote and unreal
它变得越来越遥远和不真实
There was Yacob, his master
有雅格布,他的主人
he was a kindly man when not annoyed
当他不生气时,他是一个善良的人
there was Pedro, Yacob's nephew
还有雅各布的侄子佩德罗
and there was Medina-sarote
还有麦地那-萨罗特
she was the youngest daughter of Yacob
她是雅各布最小的女儿
she was little esteemed in the world of the blind
她在盲人的世界里很少受到尊重
because she had a clear-cut face
因为她有一张清晰的脸
and she lacked any satisfying glossy smoothness
而且她缺乏任何令人满意的光泽光滑度
these are the blind man's ideal of feminine beauty
这些是盲人对女性美的理想
but Nunez thought her beautiful at first sight
但努涅斯一见钟情就觉得她很漂亮
and now she was the most beautiful thing in all the world

现在她是世界上最美丽的东西
her features were not common in the valley
她的特征在山谷中并不常见
her closed eyelids were not sunken and red
她紧闭的眼睑没有凹陷和发红
but they lay as though they might open again at any moment
但它们躺在地上，仿佛随时可能再次打开
she had long eyelashes, which were considered a grave disfigurement
她的睫毛很长，被认为是严重的毁容
and her voice was weak compared to the others
与其他人相比，她的声音很弱
so it did not satisfy the acute hearing of the young men
因此，它不能满足年轻人敏锐的听力
And so she had no lover
所以她没有情人
Nunez thought a lot about Medina-sarote
努涅斯对麦地那-萨罗特想了很多
he thought perhaps he could win her
他想也许他可以赢得她
and then he would be resigned to live in the valley
然后他会辞职住在山谷里
he could be happy for the rest of his days
他可以在余生中快乐
he watched her whenever he could
只要有可能，他就看着她
and he found opportunities of doing her little services
他找到了为她做小事的机会
he also found that she observed him
他还发现她观察了他
Once at a rest-day gathering he noticed it
有一次在休息日的聚会上，他注意到了这一点
they sat side by side in the dim starlight

他们并排坐在昏暗的星光下

the music was sweet and his hand came upon hers
音乐很甜美，他的手落在了她的手上

and he dared to clasp her hand
他敢于握住她的手

Then, very tenderly, she returned his pressure
然后，她非常温柔地回应了他的压力

And one day they were at their meal in the darkness
有一天，他们在黑暗中吃饭

he felt her hand very softly seeking him
他感觉到她的手非常温柔地寻找着他

as it chanced, the fire leapt just at that moment
碰巧，火就在那一刻跳跃了

and he saw the tenderness in her
他看到了她身上的温柔

He sought to speak to her
他试图和她说话

He went to her one day when she was sitting
有一天，当她坐着时，他去找她

she was in the summer moonlight, weaving
她在夏日的月光下，编织着

The light made her a thing of silver and mystery
光芒使她成为银色和神秘的东西

He sat down at her feet
他在她的脚边坐下

and he told her he loved her
他告诉她他爱她

and he told her how beautiful she seemed to him
他告诉她，在他看来，她是多么美丽

He had a lover's voice
他有情人的声音

he spoke with a tender reverence that came near to awe
他说话时带着一种近乎敬畏的温柔崇敬

she had never before been touched by adoration

她以前从未被崇拜所感动
She made him no definite answer
她没有给他明确的答案
but it was clear his words pleased her
但很明显,他的话让她高兴
After that he talked to her whenever he could
在那之后,他尽可能地和她说话
the valley became the world for him
山谷成了他的世界
the world beyond the mountains seemed no more than a fairy tale
山外的世界似乎只不过是一个童话故事
perhaps one day he could tell her of these stories
也许有一天他可以告诉她这些故事
Very tentatively and timidly, he spoke to her of sight
他试探性地、胆怯地向她讲述了视觉
sight seemed to her the most poetical of fancies
在她看来,视觉是最富有诗意的幻想
she attentively listened to his description
她聚精会神地听着他的描述
he told her of the stars and the mountains
他告诉她星星和山脉
and he praised her sweet white-lit beauty
他称赞她甜美的白光美
She did not believe what he was saying
她不相信他说的话
and she could only half understand what he meant
她只能半理解他的意思
but she was mysteriously delighted
但她神秘地高兴
and it seemed to him that she completely understood
在他看来,她完全理解
His love lost its awe and took courage
他的爱失去了敬畏,需要勇气

He wanted to ask the elders for her hand in marriage
他想向长辈们求婚
but she became fearful and delayed
但她变得害怕和拖延
it was one of her elder sisters who first told Yacob
是她的一个姐姐首先告诉雅各布的
she told him that Medina-sarote and Nunez were in love
她告诉他，麦地那-萨罗特和努涅斯相爱了
There was very great opposition to the marriage
这桩婚事遭到了非常大的反对
the objection wasn't because they valued her
反对不是因为他们重视她
but they objected because they thought of him as different
但他们反对，因为他们认为他与众不同
he was still an idiot and incompetent thing for them
对他们来说，他仍然是一个白痴和无能的东西
they classed him below the permissible level of a man
他们把他归类为男人允许的水平以下
Her sisters opposed the marriage bitterly
她的姐妹们强烈反对这门婚事
they feared it would bring discredit on them all
他们担心这会给他们所有人带来名誉扫地
old Yacob had formed a sort of liking for Nunez
老雅各布对努涅斯产生了一种好感
he was his nice, but clumsy and obedient serf
他是他的好人，但笨拙而听话的农奴
but he shook his head at the proposal
但他对这个提议摇了摇头
and he said the thing could not be
他说这不可能
The young men were all angry
年轻人都很生气

they did not like the idea of corrupting the race
他们不喜欢腐蚀种族的想法
and one went so far as to strike Nunez
其中一人甚至袭击了努涅斯
but Nunez struck back at the man
但努涅斯回击了这名男子
Then, for the first time, he found an advantage in seeing
然后,他第一次发现了看的优势
even by twilight he could fight better than the blind man
即使在黄昏时分,他也能比瞎子打得更好
after that fight was over a new order had been established
在那场战斗结束后,一个新的秩序已经建立起来
no one ever thought of raising a hand against him again
再也没有人想过要对他举手
but they still found his marriage impossible
但他们仍然觉得他的婚姻是不可能的
Old Yacob had a tenderness for his last little daughter
老雅各布对他最后一个小女儿有一种温柔
he was grieved to have her weep upon his shoulder
他很伤心,让她在他的肩膀上哭泣
"You see, my dear, he's an idiot"
"你看,亲爱的,他是个白痴"
"He has delusions about the world"
"他对世界有妄想"
"there isn't anything he can do right"
"他无能为力"
"I know," wept Medina-sarote
"我知道,"麦地那-萨罗特哭着说
"But he's better than he was"
"但他比以前好多了"

"for all his trying he's getting better"
"尽管他尽了一切努力，但他正在变得更好"
"And he is strong and kind to me"
"而且他对我很坚强和善良"
"stronger and kinder than any other man in the world"
"比世界上任何其他人都更坚强、更善良"
"And he loves me. And, father, I love him"
"他爱我。而且，父亲，我爱他"
Old Yacob was greatly distressed to find her inconsolable
老雅各布发现她无法安慰，非常痛苦
what made it more distressing is he liked Nunez for many things
更令人苦恼的是，他喜欢努涅斯的很多事情
So he went and sat in the windowless council-chamber
于是他走到没有窗户的议事厅里坐下
he watched the other elders and the trend of the talk
他观察着其他长老和谈话的走向
at the proper time he raised his voice
在适当的时候，他提高了声音
"He's better than he was when he came to us"
"他比他来找我们时好多了"
"Very likely, some day, we shall find him as sane as ourselves"
"很有可能，总有一天，我们会发现他和我们一样理智"
one of the elders thought deeply about the problem
其中一位长老对这个问题深思熟虑
He was a great doctor among these people
在这些人中，他是一位伟大的医生
he had a very philosophical and inventive mind
他有一个非常哲学和创造性的头脑
the idea of curing Nunez of his peculiarities appealed to him
治愈努涅斯的特殊性的想法吸引了他

another day Yacob was present at another meeting
另一天，雅格布出席了另一次会议
the great doctor returned to the topic of Nunez
这位伟大的医生回到了努涅斯的话题
"I have examined Nunez," he said
"我已经检查过努涅斯，"他说
"and the case is clearer to me"
"这个案子对我来说更清楚了"
"I think very probably he might be cured"
"我认为他很可能会被治愈"
"This is what I have always hoped," said old Yacob
"这是我一直希望的，"老雅各布说
"His brain is affected," said the blind doctor
"他的大脑受到了影响，"盲人医生说
The elders murmured in agreement
长老们嘀咕着表示同意
"Now, what affects it?" asked the doctor
"现在，什么影响了它？"医生问
"This," said the doctor, answering his own question
"这个，"医生说，回答他自己的问题
"Those queer things that are called the eyes"
"那些被称为眼睛的奇怪东西"
"they exist to make an agreeable indentation in the face"
"它们的存在是为了在脸上留下令人愉悦的压痕"
"the eyes are diseased, in the case of Nunez"
"在努涅斯的情况下，眼睛有病"
"in such a way that it affects his brain"
"以这样一种方式影响他的大脑"
"his eyes bulge out of his face"
"他的眼睛从脸上凸出来"
"he has eyelashes, and his eyelids move"
"他有睫毛，眼皮会动"
"consequently, his brain is in a state of constant

irritation"
"因此，他的大脑处于持续的刺激状态"
"and so, everything is a distraction to him"
"所以，一切都让他分心"
Yacob listened intently at what the doctor was saying
雅各布专心致志地听着医生在说什么
"I think I may say with reasonable certainty that there is a cure"
"我想我可以合理肯定地说，有一种治愈方法"
"all we need to do is a simple and easy surgical operation"
"我们需要做的只是一个简单易行的外科手术"
"all this involves is removing the irritant eyes"
"所有这一切都涉及去除刺激性的眼睛"
"And then he will be sane?"
"然后他会理智吗？"
"Then he will be perfectly sane"
"那么他将完全理智"
"and he'll be a quite admirable citizen"
"他将是一个非常令人钦佩的公民"
"Thank Heaven for science!" said old Yacob
"感谢上天赐予科学！"老雅各布说
and he went forth at once to tell Nunez of the good news
他立刻出去把这个好消息告诉努涅斯
But Nunez wasn't quite as enthusiastic about the idea
但努涅斯对这个想法并不那么热情
he received the news with coldness and disappointment
他带着冷漠和失望的心情收到了这个消息
"the tone of your voice does not inspire confidence"
"你说话的语气不能激发信心"
"one might think you do not care for my daughter"
"有人可能会认为你不关心我的女儿"

It was Medina who persuaded Nunez to face the blind surgeons
是麦地那说服努涅斯面对盲人外科医生
"You do not want me," he said, "to lose my gift of sight?"
"你不想让我,"他说,"失去我的视力天赋吗?"
She shook her head
她摇了摇头
"My world is sight"
"我的世界是视觉"
Her head drooped lower
她的头垂得更低了
"There are the beautiful things"
"有美丽的事物"
"the world is full of beautiful little things"
"世界上到处都是美丽的小东西"
"the flowers and the lichens amidst the rocks"
"岩石中的花朵和地衣"
"the light and softness on a piece of fur"
"一块毛皮上的轻盈和柔软"
"the far sky with its drifting dawn of clouds"
"遥远的天空,飘荡着云彩的黎明"
"the sunsets and the stars"
"日落与星星"
"And there is you"
"还有你"
"For you alone it is good to have sight"
"只有你一个人,有视力是件好事"
"to see your sweet, serene face sight is good"
"看到你甜美、安详的脸庞,视力很好"
"to see your kindly lips"
"看到你善良的嘴唇"
"your dear, beautiful hands folded together"
"你亲爱的,美丽的双手合十"

"it is these eyes of mine you won"
"是我的这双眼睛你赢了"
"it is these eyes that hold me to you"
"是这双眼睛把我抱在你身边"
"but it is these eyes that those idiots seek"
"但那些白痴寻找的正是这双眼睛"
"Instead, I must touch you"
"相反,我必须摸你"
"I would hear you, but never see you again"
"我会听到你的声音,但再也见不到你了"
"must I come under that roof of rock and stone and darkness?"
"我必须到那岩石、石头和黑暗的屋檐下吗?"
"that horrible roof under which your imaginations stoop"
"那个可怕的屋顶,你的想象力在它下面弯曲"
"no; you would not have me do that?"
"不;你不会让我那样做吗?
A disagreeable doubt had arisen in him
他心中产生了一种令人不快的怀疑
He stopped and left the thing in question
他停了下来,离开了那个东西
she said, "I wish sometimes you would not talk like that"
她说:"我希望有时你不要那样说话"
"talk like what?" asked Nunez
"像什么一样说话?"努涅斯问
"I know your sight is pretty"
"我知道你的视力很漂亮"
"It is your imagination"
"这是你的想象"
"I love it, but now..."
"我喜欢它,但现在……"
He felt cold at the gravity of her words

他对她话语的严重性感到冷淡
"Now?" he said, faintly
"现在？"他淡淡地说
She sat quite still without saying anything
她静静地坐着，什么也没说
"you think, I would be better without my eyes?"
"你以为，没有眼睛我会更好吗？"
He was realising things very swiftly
他很快就意识到了这一点
He felt anger at the dull course of fate
他对命运的沉闷过程感到愤怒
but he also felt sympathy for her lack of understanding
但他也对她缺乏理解感到同情
but his sympathy for her was akin to pity
但他对她的同情类似于怜悯
"Dear," he said to his love
"亲爱的，"他对他的爱人说
her spirit pressed against the things she could not say
她的精神压在她不能说的话上
He put his arms about her and he kissed her ear
他搂着她，亲吻她的耳朵
and they sat for a time in silence
他们静静地坐了一会儿
"If I were to consent to this?" he said at last
"如果我同意的话？"他最后说
in a voice that was very gentle
用非常温柔的声音
She flung her arms about him, weeping wildly
她搂着他，疯狂地哭泣
"Oh, if you would do that," she sobbed
"哦，如果你愿意那样做，"她抽泣着说
"if only you would do that one thing!"
"要是你愿意做那一件事就好了！"
Nunez knew nothing of sleep in the week before the

- 69 -

operation
努涅斯在手术前一周对睡眠一无所知
the operation that was to raise him from his servitude and inferiority
将他从奴役和自卑中解救出来的手术
the operation that was to raise him to the level of a blind citizen
将他提升到盲人公民水平的行动
while the others slumbered happily, he sat brooding
当其他人快乐地睡着时,他却坐在那里沉思
all through the warm, sunlit hours he wandered aimlessly
在温暖、阳光明媚的几个小时里,他漫无目的地徘徊
and he tried to bring his mind to bear on his dilemma
他试图用自己的思想来应对他的困境
He had given his answer and his consent
他已经给出了他的答案和同意
and still he was not sure if it was right
他仍然不确定这是否正确
the sun rose in splendour over the golden crests
太阳在金色的波峰上灿烂地升起
his last day of vision had began for him
他的最后一天异象开始了
He had a few minutes with Medina-sarote before she went to sleep
在她入睡之前,他和麦地那-萨罗特有几分钟的时间
"Tomorrow," he said, "I shall see no more"
"明天,"他说,"我再也见不到了。
"Dear heart!" she answered
"亲爱的心!"她回答
and she pressed his hands with all her strength
她用尽全身力气按着他的手
"They will hurt you, but little"
"他们会伤害你,但很少"

"you are going to get through this pain"
"你会度过这种痛苦的"
"you are going through it, dear lover, for me"
"亲爱的爱人,你正在经历它,为了我"
"if a woman's heart and life can do it, I will repay you"
"如果一个女人的心和生命能做到,我会报答你"
"My dearest one," she said in a tender voice, "I will repay"
"我最亲爱的人,"她用温柔的声音说,"我会报答的"
He was drenched in pity for himself and her
他沉浸在对自己和她的怜悯中
He held her in his arms and pressed his lips to hers
他把她抱在怀里,把嘴唇贴在她的嘴唇上
and he admired her sweet face for the last time
他最后一次欣赏她甜美的脸庞
"Good-bye!" he whispered to the dear sight of her
"再见!"他对着她亲爱的视线低声说
And then in silence he turned away from her
然后他默默地转身离开了她
She could hear his slow retreating footsteps
她能听到他缓慢后退的脚步声
something in the rhythm of his footsteps threw her into a passion of weeping
在他的脚步声中,有什么东西让她陷入了哭泣的激情中
He had fully meant to go to a lonely place
他本来是想去一个寂寞的地方的
to the meadows with the beautiful white narcissus
到草地上,有美丽的白色水仙
there he wanted remain until the hour of his sacrifice
他想留在那里,直到他牺牲的那一刻
but as he walked he lifted up his eyes
但当他走路时,他抬起了眼睛
and he saw the morning with his sight
他用他的眼光看到了早晨

it was like an angel shining in golden armour
它就像一个穿着金色盔甲的天使

he truly did love Medina-sarote
他真的很喜欢麦地那-萨罗特

he was prepared to give up his sight for her
他准备为她放弃视力

he was going to live the rest of his life in the valley
他将在山谷中度过余生

the angel marched down the steeps of the meadows
天使走下草地的陡峭

and it bathed everything in its golden light
它沐浴在金色的光芒中

without any notice something in him changed
不知不觉中，他身上的某些东西发生了变化

the country of the blind was no more than a pit of sin
瞎子的国度只不过是一个罪恶的深渊

He did not turn aside as he had meant to do
他没有像他想的那样转身离开

but he went on and passed through the wall
但他继续往前走，穿过了墙

from there he went out upon the rocks
从那里，他走到岩石上

his eyes were upon the sunlit ice and snow
他的眼睛注视着阳光普照的冰雪

he saw their infinite beauty
他看到了他们无限的美丽

his imagination soared over the peaks
他的想象力在山峰上翱翔

his thoughts went to the world he wouldn't see again
他的思绪去了他再也见不到的世界

he thought of that great free world
他想到了那个伟大的自由世界

the world that he was prepared to part from
他准备离开的世界

the world that was his own
属于他自己的世界
and he had a vision of those further slopes
他看到了那些更远的斜坡
his mind took him through the valleys he had come from
他的思想带他穿过了他来自的山谷
he went along the river into the city
他沿着河进了城
in his mind he could see Bogota
在他的脑海中，他可以看到波哥大
his imagination carried him through the city
他的想象力带他穿越了这座城市
a place of multitudinous stirring beauty
一个充满激动人心的美丽之地
a glory by day, a luminous mystery by night
白天是荣耀，夜晚是光明的奥秘
a place of palaces and fountains
宫殿和喷泉的地方
a place of statues and white houses
雕像和白色房屋的地方
his mind went with him out the city
他的思绪跟着他出了城
he followed the journey of a river
他跟随一条河流的旅程
the river went through the villages and forests
河流穿过村庄和森林
a big steamer came splashing by
一艘大轮船飞溅而过
the banks of the river opened up into the sea
河岸通向大海
the limitless sea with its thousands of islands
无边无际的大海及其数千个岛屿
he could see the lights of the islands and the ships

他可以看到岛屿和船只的灯光

life continued on each little island
每个小岛上的生活仍在继续

and he thought about that greater world
他想到了那个更广阔的世界

he looked up and saw the infinite sky
他抬起头，看到了无边无际的天空

it was not like the sky in the valley of the blind
它不像盲人谷的天空

a small disk cut off by mountains
一个被山隔开的小圆盘

but, an arch of immeasurably deep blue
但是，一个无比深蓝色的拱门

and in this he saw the circling of the stars
在这一点上，他看到了星星的盘旋

His eyes began to scrutinise the circle of mountains
他的眼睛开始审视那圈群山

he looked at it a little keener than he had before
他看得比以前更敏锐了

"perhaps one could go up that gully"
"也许有人可以爬上那条沟壑"

"from there one could get to that peak"
"从那里可以达到那个顶峰"

"then one might come out among those pine trees"
"那么一个人可能会从那些松树中出来"

"the slope past the pines might not be so steep"
"经过松树的斜坡可能没有那么陡峭"

"and then perhaps that wallface can be climbed"
"然后也许可以爬上那个墙面"

"where the snow starts there will be a river"
"雪从哪里开始，哪里就会有一条河"

"from there there should be a path"
"从那里应该有一条路"

"and if that route fails, to the East are other gaps"

"如果这条路线失败了，东边还有其他缺口"
"one would just need a little good fortune"
"一个人只需要一点好运气"
He glanced back at the village
他回头看了一眼村子
but he had to look at it once more
但他不得不再看一遍
he looked down into the country of the blind
他俯视着盲人的国度
he thought of Medina-sarote, asleep in her hut
他想起了麦地那-萨罗特，在她的小屋里睡着了
but she had become small and remote to him
但她对他来说已经变得渺小而遥远
he turned again towards the mountain wall
他又转向山壁
the wall down which he had come down that day
那天他倒下的那堵墙
then, very circumspectly, he began his climb
然后，他非常谨慎地开始攀登
When sunset came he was no longer climbing
当日落到来时，他不再攀登
but he was far and high up the valley
但他在山谷的远处，高高在上
His clothes were torn and his limbs were bloodstained
他的衣服被撕裂，四肢沾满血迹
he was bruised in many places
他多处瘀伤
but he lay as if he were at his ease
但他躺着，好像他很自在
and there was a smile on his face
他的脸上露出了笑容
From where he rested the valley seemed as if it were in a pit
从他休息的地方看，山谷似乎在一个坑里

now it was nearly a mile below him
现在它比他低近一英里
the pit was already dim with haze and shadow
坑里已经昏暗了，阴霾和阴影
the mountain summits around him were things of light and fire
他周围的山峰是光和火的东西
the little things in the rocks were drenched with light and beauty
岩石中的小东西被光和美丽浸透了
a vein of green mineral piercing the grey
一条绿色矿物的脉络穿透了灰色
a flash of small crystal here and there
这里和那里的小水晶闪光
a minutely-beautiful orange light close to his face
一道微微美丽的橙色光芒靠近他的脸
There were deep, mysterious shadows in the gorge
峡谷里有深邃而神秘的阴影
blue deepened into purple, and purple into a luminous darkness
蓝色加深为紫色，紫色变成明亮的黑暗
over him was the endless vastness of the sky
在他头顶是无尽的浩瀚天空
but he heeded these things no longer
但他不再理会这些事了
instead, he laid very still there
相反，他静静地躺在那里
smiling, as if he were content now
微笑着，好像他现在很满足
content to have escaped from the valley of the Blind
满足于从盲人谷逃脱
the valley in which he had thought to be King
他以为是国王的山谷
the glow of the sunset passed

夕阳的余晖过去了
and the night came with its darkness
黑夜伴随着黑暗而来
and he lay there, under the cold, clear stars
他躺在那里，在冰冷、清澈的星空下

The End
结束

and the night came with its darkness

and ice lay there under the cold dark skies

The End